Women in the Job Market

Ten Ways to Balance Work and Home

BY BARBARA LEIST NELSON

DORRANCE
PUBLISHING CO
EST. 1920
PITTSBURGH, PENNSYLVANIA 15238

The contents of this work, including, but not limited to, the accuracy of events, people, and places depicted; opinions expressed; permission to use previously published materials included; and any advice given or actions advocated are solely the responsibility of the author, who assumes all liability for said work and indemnifies the publisher against any claims stemming from publication of the work.

Dorrance Publishing Co
585 Alpha Drive
Pittsburgh, PA 15238
Visit our website at *www.dorrancebookstore.com*

ISBN: 978-1-6393-7471-7
eISBN: 978-1-6393-7524-0

Women in the Job Market

Ten Ways to Balance Work and Home

Table of Contents

Preface

The world seems to fluctuate in cycles, economic cycles, weather cycles, epidemic cycles, and population cycles. Neither animal nor human have much to do with how these cycles play out. Rather, we live through them as best we can.

Animal species, and sometimes plant species, have become extinct during these cycles. Man, because of his ingenuity and adaptability, has managed to emerge and continue the species.

The world matured over the ages, enduring ice advances and warming trends, causing animals and man to move, either to escape the cold or to take advantage of retreating ice to forage or plant in new, rich soil.

The world's population has endured several epidemics, or pandemics, over the centuries. The last major pandemic was the Spanish Flu, which ran from February 1918 through April 1920. Over five hundred million people succumbed.

In 1929 the world experienced a worldwide economic depression. On Black Thursday, October 24, 1929, stock prices began to fall, and over the next four days fell 29 percent.

The stock market crash cost investors $30 billion, the equivalent of $396 billion today. The crash cost more than all of World War I.

Now, here it is, 2021. Covid is beginning to subside, and the economy shows signs of coming out of a slump.

People are beginning to look for work; small business owners are rebuilding.

Most working people were hit hard by Covid 19, but one group was hit especially hard, and that was women.

Women experienced more job losses than men because of the number of businesses that have women as primary workers: retail, accommodation, hospitality, art and recreation, and hair and beauty.

Many of these types of businesses were closed for the worst of the pandemic or open only for limited hours or days.

Families with daycare or school-age children were hit even harder. Schools closed, and parents were encouraged to homeschool. If the family had toddlers and pre-school-age children, they were hit again.

Unless the parents had a grandmother or other relative willing to care for the children, one parent had to stay home. The obvious choice was the mother because she probably brought in the smaller paycheck.

Women were nearly three times more likely than men to be unemployed due to Covid-related childcare needs. Almost a year and a half later, many women are resigned to not going back to careers because of the extended school closings and the fact that many jobs will never be available again.

Covid-19 Has Been a Financial Crisis for Women.

For millions of households the pandemic has been a financial disaster. As early as April 2020, some sixteen million people had filed for unemployment in the space of weeks.

Black women suffered more layoffs than any other group. Over 58 percent of black women reported being laid off, furloughed, or had hours and wages cut, as compared to 31 percent of white men who experienced the same situations.

Most women have little in the way of a financial safety net. About a month is the farthest out any have for covering bare necessities. Black women fare even worse—about 36 percent, opposed to 16 percent of white men.

Job loss, reduced hours, a smaller paycheck, and reduced prospect of finding another job were big concerns for women. Paying for groceries, housing, and healthcare were worries that kept them awake at night.

Women were most affected because they are in worse financial situations than men. On average, women are paid 18 percent less than men in comparable positions. They have 30 percent less money in savings; women of color have even less. Women have maxed out during the pandemic. They also shoulder most of the domestic burden.

Mental Health of Women During Covid-19

Women have suffered from anxieties during Covid-19 because they have no control over this crisis. They cannot predict when normal life will return.

This lack of control over circumstances has caused feelings of despair, loneliness, fear of the unknown, fear of getting sick, fear of losing her job, and no hope of knowing when all this stress will be over.

All these worries are legitimate and can lead to real depression.

A survey indicated that from February to July 2020, 53 percent of women experienced anxiety and 29 percent of men experienced feelings of anxiety. Women's percentages are higher probably because they are likely to be caregivers.

Covid will not be with us forever. This is 2021, and businesses are gradually coming to life. More and more schools are opening. They cannot ignore the demand.

By the end of 2021, all Americans who want to be vaccinated against the virus should be. Eventually, people will decide that all these masks are no longer necessary. More and more jobs will be opening.

Covid has taught us some valuable lessons that can be applied to work and business as well. We have learned to be more careful about our health. We schedule regular check-ups with the doctor, the dentist, and other specialists. Top priority is keeping our surroundings neat, attractive, and clean.

Some companies are beginning to see the possibilities of flex time and allowing employees to work from home. Companies see less overhead because extensive office space can be eliminated. New technology is another feature that allows employees more ability to work from home.

Introduction

This book is designed for women in one of three situations as Covid-19 slowly slinks away and people and businesses start to put their lives back into some semblance of order.

> **First situation:** Women with children who were not working before pandemic but feel the necessity of finding work to help pay the debts they or themselves and their husbands have amassed in the past two years.

> **Second situation:** Women who had a small business but were forced to close because of a mandate and now want to reopen or start a new operation.

> **Third situation:** Women who worked for a corporation that partially closed and told their employees to work from home until further notice. They want to continue to work but in a part-home/part-office arrangement.

Women in any situation who need to find a way to make some money.

All these types are concerned about paying the bills, but they also worry about working and having time to be a mother and a spouse, and in some cases, a daughter. The ten ways for balancing work and home are found in chapters three, four, five, six, seven, eight, and eleven.

History of Job Market for Women

Back in Time

Work has not always meant the same thing to women as to men. Women have been the procreators. Without women, the species would disappear.

In ancient times, when homo sapiens were somewhat migratory, women had to keep up with the herd, so to speak. Babies were born on the run. The care of the offspring was a full-time job. Since babies came into this world completely helpless and needed years to grow into mature members of the society, man developed into family groups.

It was evident that a mother and her child needed protection until the child grew into an adult. It was the male's function to see that his family was protected and cared for.

Early division of labor had the male bringing home the food, fighting off the dinosaurs and making weapons; while the female had the babies, nurtured the family, made body coverings with animal hides, and swept out the cave.

That early construction of the family unit and division of labor stayed mostly the same for centuries. Basically, the boys were taught how to become men and learn the trades, while girls were taught the finer points of civilization: sewing, music, nurturing children.

It was necessary that the girls should marry and give fathers some financial relief. All those years, women were fine-tuning their brains for the future.

History of Women and Work

Early on, women depended upon their men to provide them with food, clothes, and shelter. There was no such thing as women in the workforce, unless prostitution was considered work.

It has only been about the past fifty years that women have been counted in the workforce. Since ancient times, women have only worked as vendors in South Asia, Africa, Central America, and a few other places.

They were called "Hawkers," and they sold all sorts of things like trinkets, flowers, tools, etc. They were paid a pittance to "hawk" these items. Some may have earned as much as three dollars an hour.

In ancient Rome, some women were hawkers. But primarily, women in Rome did not work; they were not even allowed to attend a political assembly, and if they were, by some strange reason, they were not allowed to speak. However, some women did work behind the scenes, manipulating their men to vote this way or that way.

Even in religion, their role was limited. Women had little to say or do in Judaism or Christianity. In the Bible, in the Book of Acts, there was a woman named Lydia who was a seller of purple cloth, and she was extremely rich. Purple was highly desired by people who were rich or of royalty, and they paid a high price for it. She was wealthy enough to have her own dwelling and servants.

Otherwise, the only real profession for women was prostitution. As Rome did, so did all other cultures. Nothing much changed for women throughout the Middle Ages and medieval times. In the Age of Enlightenment (ca.1650 in Europe), some scholars began to believe that women were intelligent; the only thing they lacked was education. Nothing much was done about that revelation.

By the end of the eighteenth century, women began to participate in salons and academic debates. Real education for women was still a long way off.

During the Industrial Revolution and the rise of factories, women gradually started entering the workforce, but even then, they were considered "cheap labor." Some were paid as little as three dollars a week. It was thought that anyone could be trained to do factory work.

Even though conditions were terrible, women continued to enter the workforce. After the Civil War, the number of women workers began to grow, primarily because of the loss of so many men. Some six hundred thousand men died, and many, many more were injured in that war. Women became active in unions at this time. Unions began to argue for an eight-hour day and equal pay.

Just as things were looking up for women workers, Samuel Gompers took over the AFL (American Federation of Labor). He believed women belonged at home, not out working.

Then came the Great Depression, and both women and men endured many setbacks. Huge numbers of people were laid off.

America entered World War II in December 1941, and big changes for women exploded in the work world. Six million new women workers entered the labor force.

In World War II, <u>Rosie the Riveter</u> symbolized the rise of women in the workplace. When the men came home from the war, there was a small decline of women workers, but the economy boomed after the war and there was a steady demand for workers, both men and women.

However, women continued to be held in typical "women's" jobs. Most popular positions held by women in post-war years included office work, retail sales, nursing, teaching, and other "feminine" occupations.

Then came the Civil Rights Act of 1964—and boosted women's power in the workplace.

Women in the Workforce Today:

Some seventy-two million women are in America's workforce today, and they make up 46.9 percent of the total labor force.

Still, women's salaries lag behind men's, and female growth in the labor market slowed between 2000 and 2010.

However, women are catching up in many professional occupations, such as the medical professions and as accountants. In fact, women make up 60 percent of all accountants in the US. Women have come a long way from selling trinkets to becoming doctors and accountants, but there is still plenty of room for growth.

It stands to reason that a good number of women, mostly those with small and school-age children, might be more interested in jobs that can be run from home. At least, that is a good place to start.

Online Jobs and Marketing

Online Jobs for Women

There are hundreds of jobs offered and described on the Internet. Most people can get carried away with all the offers of making big money with what appears to be little effort or background.

Numerous job offers are listed every day. In fact, new ideas pop up all the time.

It is important to realize that not everything on the Internet is a good deal or even a bona fide offer. The Internet is not for the timid or the gullible. *The old saying "If it sounds too good to be true, it probably is" should be the first thing to consider while surfing the Internet.*

Check out jobs with the Better Business Bureau, especially those that offer big money for little time spent. Keep a list of those that seem to be real.

Some job suggestions could be the beginning of a new business. A few can bring in a good chunk of money, while others will not payout very well.

Certain online possibilities need extensive experience to qualify; others just need a willingness to begin. Most need at least some marketing skills to let people know where the business is and what is being offered.

Here are just a few of the online job offerings available to women, or anyone for that matter.

Pet Sitter: This job is for people who love pets, especially cats and dogs, and know something about taking care of them. Be ready to show some credentials; after all, people are hiring a stranger to come into their house and care for their pet.

This can be expanded into a business, like doing some shopping for the family, taking care of plants, etc.

Foreign Language Translator: People who are proficient in Spanish, French, Italian, Japanese, Chinese may find work in translating recordings or documents or transcribing material.

Women have turned **running errands** and completing tasks for extra busy people into lucrative businesses. However, this type of business may not be the best choice if there are small children to take care of.

This is a business that needs someone available at all times of the day. A lot depends on the ages of the children. Elementary school-age children love to deliver things. They could help by riding with Mom after school. But be careful that they are not ever in harm's way. There are laws concerning children working.

EX: *Several years ago, when I was busy getting out reports and documents for individuals or small organizations, I hired a lady who had just such a company. She would pick up documents from me and hand deliver them to wherever I needed them to go. I even hired her to take me to the airport and pick me up on my return flight. Her service was better than calling a cab or a messenger service.*

It's not difficult to set competitive pricing and work out times for deliveries and pickups. Do some calling around, find out heavy traffic and light traffic times. Work on delivering it quicker than any competitor.

The web is overrun with companies looking for people to fill out **surveys**, and they pay for the service. Only trouble is, they pay such a small amount. These survey companies seldom pay more than a few cents per survey.

The number of surveys a week a person would have to fill out to make a few dollars is not worth the effort, in my opinion. I find it to be extremely monotonous work.

There are numerous opportunities for freelancers with writing skills: writing articles, web design, social media marketing, data entry, virtual assistant, customer service, travel consultant, etc.

People who have specialized training can oftentimes set up a business utilizing that training.

EX: For instance, *I am a musician. For some years I taught piano, voice, and accordion out of my own home. We had a spare room that I turned into a music studio, and I could teach and keep an eye on my young child. During that time, my husband was a high school teacher and he set up tutoring times for children who needed more than the regular school day could offer.*

He set up a classroom downstairs. We set up a play area for our little boy next to his classroom. I taught upstairs, he taught downstairs, and we did not have to hire a babysitter. It was an ideal set up.

To set up a business in any area, it takes some accumulated knowledge in all job categories. Spend some time brushing up on skills and workout a business plan.

This would also be a good time to do some self-assessment. Ask yourself: "Do I have a good work-on-my-own personality? Can I organize my time effectively?

"Is there a small space in the house that I can turn into an office? If my work idea does not turn out the way I hoped it would, will I just throw up my hands and quit?"

Have a little family meeting. Explain to the children and your husband what you plan to do to bring home an extra paycheck. Find out if they will do small jobs such as take out the garbage, walk the dog, set the table.

Assure your children that Mom and Dad will always be there for them regardless of where either of them is working.

Finally, what tools are needed for a home office? Probably a desk, certainly a computer, a printer, and a phone. Consider a decent chair.

Anyone who sits at a desk all day will need a comfortable chair. Is the space well lit? Is the space adequate? If the answer is a positive yes, then it is time to get serious.

One last thing needs to be done. Make some strict rules and make sure everybody abides by them. Print out the rules and mount them in a place where everyone can read them.

What is included in the rules? Hours the office is open. Hours may read like this: "Weekdays: 9 A.M. to 11.45 A.M./1 P.M. to 4 P.M. and 5 to 6:30 P.M. Saturday: 8:30 A.M. to 1:00 P.M. Holidays: closed."

Other rules may be: "Do Not Disturb except for emergencies. No personal calls during office hours." In other words, set up a professional office and run it like a professional. It does not matter whether the space is used for a start-up business or part time for a corporate office. Marketing is the next thing to do. Let everybody know. Be sure to keep good financial records.

Marketing Plans

The hard part of starting a business is working out a marketing plan. There are so many avenues available. Today's market is packed with all kinds of business enterprises that it seems that the loudest voice gets noticed and everybody else disappears.

Start with telling family members and close friends. They will not automatically remember, so keep reminding them.

Business cards are a must. They are not expensive, and they can be tucked into every letter, card, purchase. Have a business card ready to hand out at every contact.

Stationary is another must have. Find a do-it-yourself print store and print your own. A thousand is plenty to start with. Keep headings and logos simple at the beginning.

Social media is all around us. Most people have a **Facebook** account. Post information to all contacts. Open a business account with Facebook and let people know about the new business in town.

Do not stop there. Use them all: **Twitter** for short messages, **Instagram** for pictures of products. **Pinterest** takes time to learn but will give a good return. Pinterest offers both business and personal accounts. They also run an analytics report on how often a business board has visitors. **LinkedIn** is for business and professional people and allows companies and individuals the opportunity to post articles and promotions about their businesses.

Start a website and promote services and products.

Start with low cost and free advertising. Ask around. There are many places that will allow free flyers on bulletin boards.

Personal contact is powerful.

EX. *My husband and I moved around when we were first married. I taught piano and my husband was a college professor. Whenever we settled in a new city, I found out where all the music stores were and stopped by to introduce myself. Told them I was looking for students, gave them my professional background and asked them to refer anyone looking for a piano teacher to me.*

It worked. Most local teachers had as many students as they wanted. In three months, I had all the students I wanted.

Twenty years or more ago, music stores sold sheet music and lesson books. I always purchased my materials from them and often referred a prospective piano customer to them.

Personal contact is unbeatable. It is not easy, but the reward is great.

Radio and television ads bring in customers but can be expensive. Use sparingly until the business is established.

3

Managing a Home Office

A Corner to Call Her Own

No matter what the lady of the house decides to do—stay in her present position with flex time, look for a new job, or start her own business—she needs a space to call her own.

It does not have to be spacious but large enough for a computer, printer, some shelf space, a desk, and a decent chair.

A friend of mine turned a walk-in closet into her office. She had everything built in, the computer and printer, on a shelf just the right height for her to sit and work. When we had a consultation, I sat in the hall, and it worked fine.

Mom as Executive Director of the Household

Mom is busy in the mornings, what with a husband, a first grader and a fifth grader to get off to work and school.

The husband gets out early. The two children are fortunate to be on a bus line. The bus picks them up in front of their house and drops them off at school.

On the days Mom goes into the office, she drives them to school.

Somehow executive director seems to be the right title for the lady of the house. She oversees all the business of the household. Kids up and off to school, husband out the door, Mom dressed and off to work on time.

She is home after work and orchestrating the evening activities, from dinner, homework, plans for the weekend, etc. She is up at 5 A.M. and is lucky to be back in bed by 11 P.M.

Now Mom knows, from visiting with her friends, that if she intends to work from home even a couple of days a week, she needs a corner to call her own. And not just the corner of the kitchen counter but a space that will allow for the necessary office furniture and allow her the required privacy.

She considers how much room she will need and where that size can be carved out of their already packed home. She paces the house and comes up with some ideas.

The unfinished downstairs is large enough for two rooms. Her husband has been using the area as a makeshift den.

Why not have a bedroom and a den downstairs and convert one of the bedrooms upstairs for her office?

The boys can share and will enjoy having more room downstairs and being further away from Mom's close supervision. Her husband is happy with the idea of a real workspace for himself, so they consider making the changes.

Working from home is gaining in popularity since so many office workers opted to take their office home during the pandemic.

Some thirty million people—both male and female—work from home at least part of the workweek in today's workforce, and the number is expected to rise every year.

This new trend is especially good for women, who often need a flexible schedule, especially those who have small children and possibly elderly parents who may need assistance.

From Bare Room to Workplace

Whether Mom works at home two days a week or every day at home, she needs her own space. She needs to get away from whatever is going on in the rest of the house.

When the physical space has been agreed upon, it is time to transform that space into an office. It does not need to be a big space. It needs to be a workable space. A stand for a computer and a printer will be necessary unless the desk is big enough for the computer as well as writing space and the phone.

Take time to find a comfortable chair. Why all the fuss about the chair?

Because the chair is the only work chair in the office. Mom does not need an uncomfortable chair to squirm in all day.

Invest in a chair that has arms, can be adjusted up or down, and has good, firm upholstering. Material is a personal preference. Now look around the office space. It consists of four bare walls, except for the door.

Do the walls need a paint job? If so, select a soft, light color, like a pale blue or light yellow or beige, with a contrast for trim but still light or muted. Select a pleasant landscape or floral picture to decorate one wall.

Nothing can be less motivating than a dark, cluttered work area. Plan on good lighting. Be sure artificial lighting is adequate to light up the whole room.

One last consideration. People will stop by occasionally. Do not have an extra chair in the office. If there is no place to sit, they will not stay long.

The person who is at home all day controls the environment. Set the thermostat at a comfortable temperature.

Set up break times and lunch times. Everybody needs a change of pace during the day. Plan a morning coffee break, and an afternoon snack break.

Lunch time can be thirty minutes to an hour. These breaks during the day are good for the overall daily output.

A project will look much more interesting after a few minutes away.

We hear stories about a great novelist who insists that the best thing about working from home is that she can wear her PJs all day. That may work for the great novelist, but most of us need to look and act the part of a businessperson.

It is good for the psyche. So, get up and get dressed, put on the make-up, comb the hair, find a pair of comfortable shoes, and nothing will get in your way.

Some people do their best work in the morning. Others cannot seem to get up full steam until after lunch. Schedule the bulk of your work according to your own built-in timetable.

EX. I have an ancient cat that allows me to live with her so long as I adhere to her daily schedule. She gets up at 5:30 A.M., has breakfast, attends to her morning constitutional, goes back to bed, sleeps for two hours.

After two hours, she is up and repeats her schedule: eats, washes, goes back to bed, sleeps two hours, etc. That is her day.

When you consider her activity, it is not the worst schedule: working diligently in two-hour shifts with a short break in between.

The cat is on to a good thing. Each daily schedule will fluctuate with the priorities of the day. Get up and move periodically during the day. Sitting all day hunched over the computer is not good for posture, breathing, joints or eyes.

Staring at a computer screen will leave the eyes feeling blurry and gritty. Ask an eye doctor for a recommendation for eye drops that will soothe those red eyes.

Just getting up and stretching a few times, taking a few deep breaths, maybe doing a few jumping jacks will get the heart rate moving a little faster.

Sitting at the computer takes almost no exertion, which can lead to shallow breathing. Getting up and moving around just enough to start breathing a little faster will help circulation.

For some years, corporations have encouraged workers to take time for a daily workout.

Some companies have even set aside space for exercise machines and walking paths for their employees.

EX: *I worked for a large publishing company for several years. It was a building with about six or eight floors. The upper floors were used primarily for stocks, paper, and supplies.*

Management decided to commit one floor as a walking track for employees. All materials were stacked on shelves, and a track was marked for walking. If I remember correctly, six times around the track was a mile. It was well used. I hate exercise. But I made myself do it because it was available.

Set aside fifteen to thirty minutes in the daily schedule for a good workout. A regular exercise program is good for all systems of the body, and it can help maintain a healthy weight. Referring to the previous section on dressing for work every day no matter what the decisions are, it might be prudent to put on workout clothes if a workout session is on the schedule. That way there is no time wasted in changing clothes.

Another problem that keeps us from settling down to work are all those neat little snacks that somehow manage to leave the store with us on shopping day.

Snacking through the day on whatever is in the refrigerator is a bad habit and a recipe for weight gain.

Do not fall into the habit of snacking instead of eating regular meals. If the plan is to start the day at 8 A.M., then start with a good breakfast at 7 A.M.

Same thing with lunch. Stop at noon and fix lunch. Take a thirty-minute lunch and back at it at 12:30 or 1:00 P.M.

Schedule a fifteen-minute break about 10 A.M. and an afternoon break about 3 P.M. A good snack can be a granola bar or some fresh or dried fruit. Have a bottle of water handy for all day hydrations.

Build a Support System

Loneliness is a factor when a person works at home. For the woman working from home two days a week and three days in the corporate office, loneliness is not too big a factor, but for the lady in the home office five-plus days a week, loneliness can set in with a vengeance.

Lack of co-workers and someone to talk to can be just as unhealthy as going without food all day. We are social creatures and need human interaction.

Build a system of co-workers and friends online or in a chat room. Set up a telephone round robin. Be careful about the time factor.

Do not waste valuable work time for gossip sessions, but questions and ideas from partners online can be refreshing.

4

Better Time Management

Time is hard to manage. It tends to get away from us. Sit down to do a particular task and something else jumps out and causes a distraction.

An hour later, a completely different subject has taken over and time management is out the door.

The question is how to exercise management skills and stay on track. Time management can be mastered with a little practice. It means putting on blinders and exercising tremendous self-control.

Time management for work-at-home moms is extremely important if they are to be successful at running a business.

Scheduling

A schedule means different things to different people. To some it means one thing in the morning, something else in the afternoon, and maybe just OUT in the evening. To a businessperson, that kind of schedule would mean nothing. A work schedule should be detailed enough to allow a smooth transition from one task to the next.

Some people like to make a monthly schedule. Others will rely on a daily schedule. Daily schedules tend to get messy by the end of the month. A better suggestion would be to make a monthly skeleton schedule, then fill in each week as the month progresses.

If there are pre-school children at home, schedule intense work during the children's afternoon naptime. That will provide an hour or two to take care of work that needs a quiet time and undivided attention.

If there are all school-aged children in the home, then Mom is doubly blessed with a good portion of the day uninterrupted.

Scheduling, with a heartbeat's chance of being followed, gets better as the children get older. Make sure that adequate time is scheduled to finish a job. For instance, if a task can be finished in thirty minutes, schedule forty-five minutes.

At the end of the day, if there is unfinished work left to be done, put those tasks at the top of the next day.

By the end of the week, if the daily schedule is followed diligently, there should not be any carryover tasks into the next week.

Multitasking

Multitasking means performing several things at the same time, like a computer. Well, human beings do not operate with the efficiency of a computer, but moms can manage several things at the same time; that is why they are labeled busy moms.

The trick here is to schedule for work and schedule for home and children. A lot of people carry over work into home hours. If work and home have been scheduled correctly, then one should not careen into the other.

Set up a daily routine but stay creative. Routines are made to be changed. If there is a daily routine, even though sometimes it must be rearranged, people will fall back into that routine and realize that the time has been managed well after all.

The secret to better time management is flexibility.

Use Tools Effectively

The Internet, computers, smartphones, tablets, etc. are indispensable in all phases of daily life, the home, and the workplace.

The trick is to manage these devices so they do not rule the day. Stay on target when researching material for an article or sales brochure.

It is so easy to stray and start looking at subjects that have nothing to do with the original material on the research list.

Email is one of the biggest time wasters in the toolbox. Do not get trapped.

Include times to check email during the day and do not deviate from those times. For instance, check email first thing in the morning. Allow about ten to fifteen minutes to answer, delete, etc.

Check again around noon and take about twenty minutes to answer any messages. Check again at the end of the workday and answer any email that has come in. Time spent is about an hour of the day for emails.

Embrace a certain routine for each day and try to stick with it. There will be things that have to be done on Monday and Wednesday, reports must go out on Thursday or Friday.

A routine guarantees that everything is done on time, in time.

Know Yourself

What has this got to do with time management? Take a moment and honestly decide if handling a work-at-home business is something that you would be happy doing, or would you be miserable and end up failing?

Takes all kinds of personalities to operate in the work world. Maybe you would be happier if someone else took care of the office details while you operated the machinery. Now is the time to find out.

Staying Motivated While Working from Home

Motivation—That is what it all comes down to, doesn't it? Motivation is what pushes us to start and finish a project. I suspect that the amount of motivation it takes to move us depends upon the task before us.

EX: *A friend calls and says she is going shoe shopping, and would I like to go with her? My answer is, "Where can I meet you and what time?"*

As you might guess, I am easily motivated to go shoe shopping. I have at least twenty pairs of shoes in all colors and styles in my closet.

What about the work waiting for me in my office? "I'll stay up late and work on it. I can catch up."

Another friend calls up and says, "I'm starting an exercise class at the Y. Would you like to come with me? It's only a six-week course."

19

You can probably guess my answer. "Oh. No, I am involved with so many things right now. I really cannot. Maybe next time, okay? But thanks for asking."

Many people are interested in having their own business and the prospect of possibly making a big income. They are motivated to be their own boss and live their own life without any constraints.

That is until they realize how much work it is and possibly how long it will take to realize a profit. That is when the motivation begins to dwindle.

A lot of women lost their job, their business, their income when Covid-19 hit the US. Perhaps the man of the house lost income as well. Everybody must bring in income so the family can survive.

Dad has a new job, but it does not pay well enough to catch up with back payments on the mortgage and credit card bills. This mom has decided; with her teaching degree, instead of returning to the classroom, she can start a business of her own.

A Business Plan

She has decided to set up a tutoring service. The couple's children are six and nine, and she is qualified to teach elementary grades.

Schools are not set up to open until fall. She knows a lot of children have fallen behind and she can use her office space for an office and classroom.

(Setting up an office, a place of her own p.11)

Now that Mom has decided what she is going to do, how does she stay motivated? She knows her subject.

She is not sure how many pupils she will have, but she will have to arrange her office space to allow for one or two students at a time and still have some room to operate.

In this instance, office time and teaching time will fluctuate. However, it is important to set a regular beginning and ending time for the workday.

Set up a daily schedule of open and closing times. For instance, workday begins at 8 A.M. and closes at 4:30 P.M. So, be ready to work at 8 A.M. and plan to close at 4:30. Do not spend the first hour in the office reading the morning paper or reading emails.

Tutoring times likely will be scheduled from noon through early evening.

How to Dress: Dress for success, no pajamas. It stands to reason that businesspeople will come to the office upon occasion. Parents will drop off children. So, be dressed for a regular business day.

Have a business plan. A business plan is a road map of business objectives, how to make money, a budget, contacts, where to be in six months, a year, etc., how much travel, when to hire help, a daily schedule, and more.

Keep social media, the phone, and email under control. These are necessary tools for business, but they can eat away the hours in a day.

A lot of stress is involved in starting a business, and there are times when it's necessary to get away for a while. Get out of the house. Plan a lunch with a friend. Socialize with a few friends occasionally.

Set up an exercise program. A program that can be utilized both at home and away. Set aside a few minutes each day to do some stretching exercises.

Sign up for an exercise program at the Y. Increasing circulation and stretching muscles and joints is good for the body's general health. Feeling good physically makes it easier to stay motivated. (More detail on exercise in chapter five.)

Staying Productive

Is there a difference between being motivated and being productive? Yes, definitely. A better way to distinguish the two is to consider them as twins. Without motivation, there is no productivity. To boost productivity, some of the same tips to boost motivation will also boost productivity. So many distractions can get in the way of productive work. Identifying some to those distractions will increase productivity.

Clean Up Clutter

At the end of each day, clear everything off the desk that is not relevant to tomorrow's work. Nothing slows motivation and productivity more than being greeted with a cluttered desk.

Take care of things as soon as possible every day. Do not carry over daily activities unless it is a necessity.

Answer mail and emails, file papers away, throw out notes that are no longer needed, move magazines and newspapers out of the way. Keep workspace clear.

Look around the office at the end of the day to see if everything is ready for work tomorrow.

EX: I like to straighten up before I leave in the evening. Others would rather make their escape and worry about clearing the way the next morning. Personally, I think leaving the clutter for the next morning is counterproductive.

Invariably, too much time is wasted on things that should have been done the day before.

Keep Kids and/or Pets Otherwise Occupied

Pets are a little easier to settle down or otherwise occupy themselves than children. Feed the dog and cat first thing in the morning and then take the dog for a long walk or run in the morning to wear down some of his energy. Dad and the children can help with this activity.

After food and a long walk, the dog will settle down for a long nap. For cats, breakfast and a few minutes of play will send her off for a nice nap.

After the pets are down and the children are off to school, there is a sizeable space to get some work done. Let us assume the first thing on the calendar for today is an article, and it is due tomorrow. A two-hour window in the morning will finish that.

School-age children will leave a sizeable amount of time to schedule work or errands before they get home in the afternoon. For toddlers, plan to work around their naps during the day.

When the children are up from naps, they might be able to help some in the office. By doing what? Well, be a little creative. Children like to move stuff around. Have them take out the trash. Put food down for the cat and the dog.

If the children are old enough to understand the importance of doggie walks every day, they should be trustworthy enough to take the dog for a walk in the afternoon and feed the cat and dog for evening.

They are learning responsibility and will have the pets out from underfoot.

Children can help with the evening meal, too. Getting things out of the refrigerator and out of the pantry, Setting the table, getting out the eating utensils, pouring the water, etc.

Turn Off Sounds and Notifications

This may sound like a silly suggestion, but think about it for a minute. Nearly all our devices "talk" to us. The phone is so irritating. It rings and announces, "You have one missed call," "One voicemail," "You have five unheard messages." It keeps on reporting until it is answered or turned off.

These messages are certainly a distraction. They keep on announcing until something is done—either answer or turn it off.

Finish one task, then take time to check messages and emails. It does save time.

Prioritize the To-Do List

Put the biggest, most complicated task first. Link similar tasks together. If there is filing to do, save it and do a batch at one time.

EX: *Years ago when I worked at a radio station, I had tons of material to file: news reports, news programs, who would report on what, guests for talk shows, etc. I put every item or report that was ready to be filed on top of the file cabinet.*

When the stack got rather high, I would schedule a time in my day for filing, usually in late afternoon. That way when I was through filing, it was time to go home. I admit it, filing is boring, and at least for me, I get braindead when I file.

Time Out the Day

For large projects, figure out how long it will take from research to finish and set aside that much time to work uninterrupted for each. Take an estimated guess at how long it will take to finish a problem.

Set aside that much time for completion and then move ahead with it. After it is finished, take a short break.

Scheduling two or three uninterrupted portions of the day, with a short break between, will accomplish a lot and still leave our busy mom alert for the evening.

Take some time out to think of ways to increase productivity. Kick back and think about ways to make the work hours more productive.

5

Weight Loss for Working Moms— The Never-Ending Battle

One of the big problems for both men and women in the United States workforce is extra pounds. If workers sit at a desk for eight hours a day, gaining weight is usually the outcome.

It is a never-ending battle. Some adults are in a continuous struggle with calories.

Sitting at a desk, in front of a computer, cranking out reports, taking information and sorting it through the computer is the formula for gaining excess pounds.

Without a certain amount of physical activity to burn off calories, our bodies add pounds. It takes both exercise and diet to shed those unwanted pounds.

Exercise

Like everything else in the workday, workers should schedule a daily exercise program.

Weight-loss for work-at-home moms take some special considerations. Exercise can be done at home, but setting up a regimen for home is so easy to forget or to put off for another day. Why not look at some other ideas?

Look around the neighborhood. Is there a gym close by? Is it within walking distance? If so, that is the best scenario. Incorporate the exercise program to include walking to and from the gym. Visit the gym and set up a program to meet your needs.

Be a Morning Exerciser

Starting the day with exercise will wake up the body and give momentum to start the daily work schedule. For those who are not accustomed to exercise, start slowly. Walking is good exercise and will burn calories along with a reduced diet.

After a few days of a brisk morning walk, start out with a walk, then start to jog. Then add running. Running is good cardio exercise.

If boredom sets in, try interval running, that is, speed up for a few minutes, then drop back to a run, then speed up and drop back etc. While at the gym, do some jump rope. A 140- pound woman can actually burn three-hundred-plus calories in thirty minutes.

After gaining stamina from walking, running, jumping rope, try spinning. Most gyms have stationary bikes, and spinning can burn a lot of calories and build up endurance.

In fact, all this exercise is burning calories and waking up the metabolism.

What is metabolism? Basal metabolism is the minimal energy expended for the maintenance of respiration, circulation, muscle tone, body temperature, glandular activity, and other vegetative functions of the body.

To put that in plain English: A person who sits still all day will not burn very many calories. If that same person eats three meals a day laden with calories, she most likely will add pounds.

If that person exercises every day, the metabolism increases, and the excess calories are burned off. That is how it works. It is the old give and take.

Some people who begin a program of weight loss, after a few days, find that they feel better and have more energy. They are wide awake and ready to tackle the agenda for the day.

Those who start a weight-loss program should have some idea of what their ideal weight should be. A person's body mass index (BMI) is a good measure of what the ideal weight should be. The BMI is a measure of body fat used to help determine whether a person is underweight, thin, ideal, overweight, obese. Height (in inches) and weight calculates a person's BMI.

I used my own numbers for this example: Height: 62" Weight: 157 lbs. BMI is=28.7. My normal healthy weight should calculate between a BMI of 18.5 – 24.9. Looks like I am a little overweight.

(If you want to find out more, you can search ideal weight Calculator SPOTEBI.)

When Do We Eat?

Exercise will not get rid of pounds by itself. The food consumed is the second component of a weight-loss program.

Here are some general rules to remember on the consumption side.

1. Keep track of calories. This is necessary to know exactly what and how much is consumed. (Find an app that will help calculate calories and portions.)
2. Hide unhealthy and calorie-laden snacks. Put healthy snacks out such as fruit, veggie snacks, nuts.
3. Do not skip a meal. Eat three meals a day. Skipping a meal may trigger overeating at the next mealtime.
4. Plan meals carefully. Plan for just a week ahead.

Here is a sample meal plan for a week:

Breakfast: hot cereal with fruit, an egg (any way you like) with an English muffin/or high-fiber cereal with a side of fruit.

Lunch: soup and salad, or sandwich and salad, or just a salad

Dinner: (more complicated because it is the whole family)

For maybe three nights: a protein, vegetable, and rice or corn

For one night, have breakfast for dinner: Turkey bacon or breakfast steaks and eggs and hashbrowns.

For one night: Try the local farmer's market. Many will cook what you choose.

Leftovers for one or two nights, and maybe just a family night out once a week.

If anyone is allergic to any foods, adjust the menus accordingly.

Meal Plans

Check out diet plans that are on the market. They are designed to take the hassle out of deciding which foods to eat and how to count calories.

I am not endorsing any plans; I am just suggesting a couple that have been on the market for years and have good reputations. **Before beginning any diet plan, check first with your doctor.**

Weight Watchers: There are a number of diet plans that Weight Watchers offer. The new WW Freestyle plan is a revised plan of the original and is an extremely popular plan that assigns points to foods that are counted each day. It might be easier to count points than to count calories.

There is also a seven-day diet plan that jumpstarts the user on a diet. It is a proven plan but may be a bit overwhelming for beginners.

WW has many plans available; beginners just need to narrow down their choice to what fits their lifestyle.

Weight Watchers holds group meetings that offer support during the dieting journey. Many successful dieters swear by the WW programs.

Nutri System: Another diet plan that has been around for many years. It is a plan that offers pre-packaged foods—the ultimate in convenience. The food is delivered to your door. There is nothing to fix and nothing to count.

Everything is marked, pre-counted, and prepackaged. The popular twenty-eight-day program offers a complete prepackaged food plan.

They also have several food plan variations. Recently, Nutri-System has advertised a plan for men and a plan for couples, as well as a shake program promising to take off eighteen pounds in two weeks.

Mediterranean Lifestyle: Another food system I would like to suggest is not really a diet plan. It is a lifestyle, eating what is grown in the countries that surround the Mediterranean Sea.

Foods include fish, produce (fruits and vegetables), whole grain, and fats from olives. Nutritionists suggest that this style of eating is especially good for the heart. Some say that it is good for diabetics.

It was also noted that some on this regimen lost weight. It is recommended that those who adhere to this food plan eat five to ten servings of vegetables a day.

The Mediterranean Plan focuses on fish and eggs, some dairy, seeds, nuts, and legumes, olives and olive oil, whole grains, herbs, and spices for seasonings.

Stay away from sugar-sweetened beverages such as sodas. Go light on candy, ice cream, and table sugar.

Also stay from refined grains such as white bread, refined wheat products, trans-fats, refined oils, processed meats, highly processed foods. Rarely eat red meat.

One or two glasses of red wine a day is acceptable. A regimen of physical activity completes the Mediterranean eating plan.

Losing weight and reviewing eating habits is quite a rigorous program, but by sliding into it gradually, it will seem less difficult.

6

Transportation: How Many Cars in the Family?

When two singles become a couple, it takes time to sort out what each one keeps and what goes out in the trash. In today's hectic world, it is reasonable to assume that both members of this new couple have their own cars.

It is also reasonable to assume that they each want to keep their cars.

A car is a sign of independence; neither one needs to ask permission of the other to grab the car keys and go. This arrangement is usually acceptable until one wants to get rid of his or her car.

The decision may depend upon how each one gets to and from work. If the couple lives in a metropolitan area with mass transit, perhaps they can get to and from work on public transportation, and in the interest of saving money, they can get rid of the car that uses more gas and needs a new engine.

When the family begins to grow, then it may be time to shop around for a good, reliable family car. When the family includes two or three children and the family dog, a good, reliable car is not a luxury; it is a necessity.

As the children grow, there are so many things that need attention that cannot be done easily with mass transit.

One child is in nursery school, the other one in kindergarten; they get out of school at different times. The food list gets longer, and when a day has been particularly long and frustrating, a late trip to the all-night grocery is much safer in a good car.

Now the question becomes who drives the family car and who is left with the old "clunker."

This may sound prejudicial, but the logical suggestion would be that mom drives the reliable family car because she is most likely the one who picks up the children from school and stops by the grocery or drugstore or both on the way home.

Dad can drive the old "clunker" because if he has car trouble, he may be the one capable of "babying" the thing home or to the car shop.

Eventually, Dad will decide that it probably would be cheaper to go ahead and trade in the old "clunker" for a reliable, easy on the gas mileage run-about.

Americans are in love with their cars. Just look at all the beautiful automobiles that are produced every year with the latest gadgets and the best in gas mileage. There is justification for this love of cars.

This is a broad and expansive country that just begs to be seen through the windows of a car. In many places in this country, there is no other way to get around except by car.

A car is a big item in the family budget, and the question always comes down to luxury or economics. A little of both would seem right. There will be times when one car is low on gas or needs a new tire or something else.

In these instances, the other car gets tapped for the outing. Both cars should always be ready for service, especially if there are children in the family.

7

Managing Family and Work

Caring for Elderly Parents While Working

Elderly parents do not always understand what their children are doing in the cutthroat world of making money. They see their daughter home some days, gone somedays, and it makes them very curious.

They cannot keep up with her schedule. What would they do if they had an emergency?

Their daughter is getting a whiff of their concerns as well. She is beginning to pull some of their records. She intends to set up a health folder for both her mom and dad.

Everything pertaining to their health: medications, doctor's appointments, directions for use of some of their new medications, exercise programs, what foods to avoid, wills, power of attorney, health directives, who to contact, which hospital to go to.

This may be time consuming, but when an emergency happens, it will save a lot of time finding papers, instructions, etc.

Set up a daily schedule for parents as well as for husband and children. Have schedules posted or filed where everybody knows where they are.

Take time every day to contact parents. It does not have to be some elaborate thing—a simple phone call will do.

EX: *I remember as my parents got older and became more isolated because of transportation and health issues, that daily phone call was the most important event of their day.*

Take Them Out

My dad loved to go out and eat. This was his special treat. Mom not so much. Their main meal was at noon.

So, if I took Dad out to lunch, that meant that Mother would not have to prepare a full meal for both. Mom preferred to snack for lunch and prepare a light supper.

I made it a part of my regular schedule to go visit them every Friday evening. They expected me to come. Sometimes I brought supper, but most of the time I ate before I came. I never stayed more than an hour. That arrangement was exactly right for all of us.

We arranged for special occasions and family events. Wherever they wanted to go, I would plan to pick them up or meet them there. These were always scheduled in advance, so I could schedule or reschedule my work.

They usually went to church on Sundays. Dad maintained his car and drove until he was ninety-three. Then I became their chauffeur. I cut back on my hours a bit, but I always maintained a daily and weekly schedule.

In their younger years, my parents traveled all over the western and southern states. But as the years bore down on them, they became homebodies.

If parents are in good health, encourage them to travel a bit. They do not have to do the travel trailer and camping thing; there are cruises, bus trips, train trips.

Encourage them to get involved in community affairs, social gatherings, and maybe even politics. The interaction between people with various ideas can be stimulating.

Involve Them with the Grandchildren

Most grandparents have one gripe. They do not see their grandchildren often enough. Grandparents are wonderful people for young children to be around, to learn from, to play with, and occasionally to stay with.

EX: *When I was a preteen, during summer vacation I would spend a week with my grandparents. I loved it. I think they did, too. Now, we all lived in the same town— about fifteen minutes away, but it might have been fifteen hours away as far as I was concerned.*

I was away from home, but I felt safe because I was with my grandparents. Other times, my grandmother would "babysit" me while my mother went shopping.

These can be precious times, for both children and parents. Such an arrangement can be beneficial for the working mom, too. There may be extenuating circumstances, but in most cases, it can be helpful and rewarding for everybody.

Acquaint Parents with Technology

Instead of having a "take your child to work day" have a "take your parent to work day." If they are having trouble understanding the whole work-at-home concept, take them to work. Let them see a modern workday at the office.

Let them see how a modern-day office is equipped and what kinds of materials can be produced and see new trends in business. Show them the future of business and the wonderful things technology can do.

They might be impressed with what they see. Suggest that they might like to get a computer to keep in touch with family and friends and explore the wonders of the world.

Consider a Caregiver

Most older adults prefer to stay in their own homes as long as feasible. However, illness and frailty may be more than they and family members can manage. When that happens, it is time to discuss hiring a caregiver.

Explain how a caregiver can take care of housekeeping and personal things for them. It will allow them to stay at home longer.

They may want to start with someone who will do the house cleaning, laundry, and grocery shopping. Later, they may need help with personal care. Always include everyone in the conversation.

It is most important that frail parents know who is coming to their home and why they are coming. They may need a reminder occasionally.

Consider the needs of elderly parents as a normal part of lifestyle changes in the family. That will make it easier to adapt work habits and schedules.

Let all members of the family know that there may be changes in the daily routine and that they may have to help in some circumstances. That way, there will be no surprises and no grumbling.

Realize that the daily schedule may need constant revision. Plan for several scenarios.

Playtime for Mom and the Children

Most work-at-home women have children at home as well as in school, and they are struggling to grow a business while being a mom, too. Being a businesswoman does not mean that she must forfeit her role as mother.

It means that she will have to figure out a way to grow her business and be a mom to growing children.

If the children are all in school, Mom will have a whole morning to get a lot of work done and be ready to take a break when the children come home.

Time-Out for Exercise

A half-hour set aside for some fun exercise and playtime will be good for Mom and the kids. If the weather is nice, plan a playtime outside.

For exercise, just do some marching in place, then jumping jacks, some twists from one side to the other, bend at the waist and touch toes without bending the knees.

Play some "circle games" like "Ring Around the Rosey," "The Hokey-Pokey," and others. Schedule the afternoon game time for no longer than thirty minutes.

That will be enough. The kids will be tired, and Mom has gotten a "second wind" for the last two or three hours of work.

Moving around, taking a few minutes to do some easy exercises will increase the blood circulation system. After a few minutes of exercise, the body will be ready to get back to work.

Anyone who has a desk job is encouraged to get up once or twice in the morning and do some stretching exercises. A ten-minute light workout will be enough to wake up the brain and invigorate the body. Repeat in the afternoon.

Pictures and Cards to Make for Family

Another project for Mom and the kids is to make birthday cards for family members. The kids can do this while Mom is working. Get out some colored paper, have some magazines around, and let the creative juices flow.

Take a piece of colored paper and show them how to fold it first one way and then the other to make a greeting card. Take the pictures the children have cut out and begin to put things together randomly.

With a little glue and some letter work by Mom, they will have some cute birthday cards for aunts, uncles, and grandpa and grandma.

Almost any card store will have colored paper, stickers, craft books, crayons, and coloring books that all kids love. And now that adult coloring books are available, both Mom and kids can spend a few minutes coloring together.

Mom has been rejuvenated, and the children have spent quality time with her. No need to feel guilty about working and ignoring the kids.

There may be times when school projects will take parental assistance and both parents will be involved in some school projects and meetings.

Date Night Ideas for Mom and Dad

A work-at-home business is a serious endeavor. It is much harder to be successful at a business from home because of so many interruptions.

A neighbor notices someone is home and comes over to borrow a cup of sugar (does anybody do that anymore?) and wants to gossip forever. The spouse and some friends call you at home. Retired parents cannot understand why there is so little time to spend with them. And then, there are those other pitfalls.

The kitchen is close by. It is so easy to stop for a mid-morning snack. Finally, there is only plain procrastination.

Few women-owned businesses make it without the full support of their spouse or significant other. No matter what the business is or how much time needs to be devoted to growing it, couples need time just for themselves. Her parents are in good health and would love to babysit their grandchildren on an afternoon.

There are some things that couples should be doing together as a family. Family life is more than the daily go to work, come home, eat dinner, put the children to bed, watch TV routine.

Mom set aside the work schedule for a few minutes and began to put together some date night ideas.

The best thing she had always liked about her husband was that he was perfectly content to just sit together and talk for hours.

It seemed that they never ran out of ideas that interested both of them. So many ideas, great ideas, silly ideas, someday ideas.

Why was it that after marriage and kids, couples seemed to let the things that brought them together fall by the wayside? This mom decided to make every effort not to let that happen to this family.

After all, children need to see that their parents love each other, and even though they both worked hard, there would always be plenty of family time.

She decided to plan some "stay-at-home" dates. During the week, the children were down by eight o'clock. She usually worked for an hour of two after that. Sometimes her spouse brought work home, too. Well, that would change, at least for one night a week.

The weather was nice now, and the evenings were not too cool to sit outside. They had a perfectly good patio, and it was time to enjoy it more often than Memorial Day, Father's Day, 4th of July, and Labor Day.

Their first date night at home was delightful, and her spouse said, "We have to do this again."

Mom had made sure that their favorite wine was well chilled, and after the children were safely in bed, they went out on the patio, sat where they could see the stars, and talked about everything that came to mind.

They even tried to name the stars and constellations. He wanted to know how she was doing getting her tutoring classes up and running.

She was just getting started and only had about three students so far. She said she had two or three more that were still thinking about it.

Her husband talked about his work, too. Then they drifted into all sorts of subjects until the wine was finished and it was late.

They both would be a little sleepy tomorrow, but their little date at home on the patio was counted as a success and many more would follow.

Dinner out was a little harder to plan for than the "spur of the moment" home dates. They both gave up the spontaneous dinner idea, because Mom was always fussing about having nothing to wear. Dad usually did not want to dress up at all.

So, dinner dates became special-occasion dates. Only the restaurant was kept secret. Mom's and Dad's birthdays were special nights out for just the two of them. However, for the children, the parents' birthdays were special family parties.

Other family birthdays and traditional holidays were always special events for the whole family. This year, the family Thanksgiving was especially festive because Mom had signed up several students and she was so thrilled.

Then there were the annual dinner parties for work, church, and other special occasions. They always planned to make these events if possible. It was an opportunity to be together all dressed up and on their best behavior to honor their life-partner.

Special Affairs Nights and Mini Vacations

Special affairs, charity nights for some great cause, were getting beyond their reach. They were required to be dressed to the nines, and they were always squeezed for a sizable donation.

The family was okay financially, but their budget did not include large donations and fancy clothes for causes that did not appeal to them.

But mini vacations for a couple of days somewhere nearby was a great way to rejuvenate the whole family.

During the summer, when the children were out of school, it was much more sensible than trying to take a two-week marathon that wore everybody to a frazzle. They planned a couple of short weekend trips during school vacation, and nobody was tired when they got back, and Mom even took her laptop with her on one occasion.

Finances, Who Maintains the Checkbook?

The one thing that young couples never seem to talk about before marriage is finances. Who is going to pay the bills? Who holds the checkbook? How to set aside money for a house someday. This is the one conversation that every couple should have before two become one.

In the aftermath of Covid-19, finances will have to be addressed, especially if the mom decides to start her own business.

Eventually, when money starts coming in from her business, she will have to open a business account, and that account will have to be her sole concern. As the business grows, she will probably need the services of an accountant.

There are companies that simply offer accountant services that are considerably less expensive than hiring a full-time employee. If the business is growing, this may be the time for Dad to take over the household finances.

Be sure this is a joint venture. Both parties must agree about how the finances will be handled. If Dad is handling the household expenses to leave Mom free to manage the business expenses, be sure that both agree. Do not mix the two sources of money.

It may have been an extra busy week, and it would be easier to throw everything together and sort it out later. Trouble is, later may not come, or when the time does come to settle out what is business and what is personal, too many things can be forgotten. Better to never let it happen in the first place.

The owner should set up the amount she will take out of the business as her salary either weekly or monthly.

If the business is profitable, she needs to calculate what percentage she will return to the business and how much for advertising, how much for inventory, how much for expansion, how much for an additional employee, how much for insurance.

The finances for the household and the finances for Mom's business are both equally important. Someday the children will want to go to college, and someday both Mom and Dad will want to retire.

The financial health of the family depends upon both Mom and Dad working together to grow their wealth.

EX: *My parents married at the end of the Great Depression. Nobody had any money. My father was making fifteen dollars a week when they married.*

My mother never worked outside the home. My father said to her that it was his responsibility to bring home the money, and she would take care of the home and children. Now let me be clear about this arrangement. Mom was fine with it. She did not want to work outside the home. And that was how they managed it for seventy-four years.

But that did not mean that my mom had no say in the finances. She had control of the checkbook. She paid the monthly bills. They also set aside, in a savings account, money for big things: a house, an appliance when an old one wore out, a better car, etc.

It was Dad who talked to financial people and set up accounts. Mom could buy whatever she wanted, and Dad could buy whatever he wanted. They both knew the limitations of their spending.

Neither one had a separate account of their own. They did have a credit account or two, but they never carried over a balance, unless the stove went out and they had to buy a new one.

Then, the one policy they adhered to kicked in. They never bought another big item until they paid off the last one. That was their financial plan. It worked for seventy-four years.

Obviously, that kind of financial plan is outdated and would bring laughter and scorn in today's world. But it worked then. It worked for them.

That is what every couple should do. Sit down together and work out a plan for taking care of the family finances.

Honor that plan until it needs to be amended. Then, sit down and work out a new plan.

From the very beginning, make out a weekly budget. It can be simple: income in one column and outgo in another column and try to balance it.

If something big comes along that must be paid for immediately, decide how to do it, add it to your credit, or take it out of the savings. Then figure out how soon the money can be replaced.

One of the biggest things that happens is that the credit card balance skyrockets and you are paying a big interest fee that is eating up your income.

It does not matter who takes care of the monthly bills, just be sure it is a joint decision. Each person may have their own checkbook and credit card(s). Just be sure there is agreement on how things are to be paid.

Set up a savings account for that home you both want someday, and anything else that will take a bundle of money. An education fund for the children's college is another wise move.

It does not matter how you plan to take care of the money—just be sure it is done together. When it is time to set up a portfolio for retirement, be sure it is set up together.

New Normal for the Corporate Office—Hybrid Strategy

When Covid-19 hit the workplace in 2020, many offices closed and sent their workers home to work.

Consequently, most workers have decided that they like working from home, and corporations found out that production from employees remained almost the same. A new workplace model is being developed that both corporations and workers are approving.

Hybrid Workplace

According to a recent survey by Slack, just 12 percent of workers want to return to the office full time. Data from a survey of over nine thousand workers in the US, UK, France, Germany, Japan, and Australia discovered that only 12 percent want to go back to work entirely in an office.

The majority of workers, 72 percent, want to continue with what is being labeled as a hybrid work style.

This has huge implications for workforce management, or capital investments, in a physical office versus a digital infrastructure.

Hybrid Workstyle Leads to Better Workplace Satisfaction.

A majority of workers, 51 percent, report improved work/life balance from remote work with only 17 percent declining.

More compelling is that workers say that over all workplace satisfaction is at 45.8 percent while only 20 percent report a drop in overall satisfaction.

Apparently, more people are happy with working from home. Other surveys concur with Slack's research.

IBM – A majority of workers, 75 percent, would like to continue the work from home.

Boston Consulting – 60 percent surveyed in the USA, Germany, and India want flexibility on when or where they work.

The desire to continue with a hybrid workplace is global. A majority have felt no change in workplace productivity.

Increased workplace satisfaction is a huge opportunity for companies. More satisfaction among employees may well drive increased profits for employers.

Hybrid workstyles, the new normal, may soon become merely normal.

The Hybrid Work Strategy

At the beginning of the pandemic, companies who sent employees home to work were worried about employee productivity and overall organizational success.

A year later, these same companies face another challenge: announcing an opening date for all employees to return to the workplace or announcing a full-time remote workplace policy.

Facebook has already moved forward with a remote work plan.

Some companies, or certain departments, have made plans toward a hybrid work model. Some employees have said "goodbye" to their former offices.

However, companies should not be too quick to shutdown HQ. To create a sustainable future, company executives should consider a hybrid approach to blend office space for collaboration with working from home for individual work.

One big loss of working from home is the level of personal interaction. Workers no longer have contact with co-workers.

To build an inclusive hybrid culture, it is critical to put the remote worker at the center of all company activities.

Remote employees stay connected to each other through chat, voice, and video collaboration.

Office workers transition from one workstation to another with lighter laptops and mobile devises.

Hybrid work will force new ways of doing the old things. Some people may decide to move from close by to the company hub or to relocate permanently.

Companies will need to make changes in pay practices, for instance.

A hybrid work strategy can be fully supported with strategic planning and technology to keep employees connected, whether they choose to be in the office or at a remote location.

Benefits may change to cover hybrid workforce needs. In a hybrid work force, managers may look at benefits differently. Managers may see their employee's homes and lives on a different level. There is the possibility that benefits for employees that work remotely will cover new benefits, such as benefits for emotional and mental health.

Benefits have expanded to address mental health and well-being issues, to incentives for redesigning home office spaces. Other possibilities might include marriage counseling.

One big hurdle for hybrid workstyles is how organizations can build and uphold employee-manager relationships.

Job Candidates Insist on Flexibility of Remote Work Areas.

Remote work allows for more flexibility managing life necessities—like childcare for instance.

More and more candidates for employment—men and women alike—will not consider a job if it does not allow for at least partial remote work.

A talent shortage has pushed employers to look at a wider variety of backgrounds for candidates, and women are showing up more often as qualified talent.

Make-up and Dress for Professional Women

This is 2021 and the competence of women in the office is still being judged by their make-up? It seems so. What the lady wears on her face cannot possibly reveal how smart and business savvy she is. Well, apparently it can.

Climbing the professional ladder has always been tricky especially for women.

Expectations on how women should look in the office have changed, but no one told women the rules. It is certainly not the well-scrubbed look.

It seems to be all about the eyelids. Now, men are not immune from being judged on their looks, but women seem to endure scrutiny beyond what men experience.

No, it is not fair, but not much in life is fair. So, what type of make-up should women strive for in the workplace? Bold? Sexy? Natural? Clean, scrubbed look?

Most women would eliminate "sexy" from that list of "looks" to aim for and head for something "au natural" or bold.

When questioned, both men and women felt that make-up made a woman appear more interesting, trustworthy, competent, likeable than the barefaced look.

So, ladies, away with the fresh-scrubbed look and on with the lipstick and mascara.

Apparently, some make-up will get a more positive response from co-workers than no make-up at all. But not every look will get positive responses in the office. Here are some guidelines.

Glamorous make-up is out of place in the work world. No "smoky eyes" unless "work" is a night club. The best approach is to minimize. Highlight the best features, but in an understated way.

Choose an eyeliner pencil instead of a liquid to soften the look; go easy when filling in the eyebrows. Use a light application of eye shadow and one coat of mascara, a quick brush of blusher, and a modest layer of lipstick or gloss. As to the shade of lipstick—red, neon pink, or sparkles are out of consideration.

The professional look is a neutral, natural one, with shades of brown, taupe, nude, light pink on the cheeks, lips, and lids, and a mascara shade that matches the natural lashes.

Other colors will work, too, if shades are light and complimentary. The entire face should look well-blended. Make sure that well-blended face will last all day. It does no good to look all streaky by noon. Use long-lasting and waterproof eye make-up.

However, by afternoon, the make-up can wear thin, so be sure to bring a mirror for a quick touch-up before a presentation.

Applying make-up takes time, whether it be light for day or bold for evening. But there are some things that can be eliminated from the office look that would be used for evening.

Do things like eyebrow tweezing during off hours and keep daily make-up to the minimum for a light look.

The make-up scene can be broken into five tips:

1. One Try - The light look may not appeal to all women, but give it a try.
2. Go Easy - Do not be heavy-handed with the application.
3. The Light Touch- Self-explanatory.
4. Last Long - Waterproof and long-lasting make-up.
5. A Quick Fix- Strike for five minutes to apply on a work morning.

Business Dress for Women

Some things have changed over the years when it comes to what is appropriate for the office and what is not. Proper attire for the office has relaxed. Slacks are now appropriate in the workplace. The pantsuit has become the "uniform" for most women for several reasons.

The jacket makes it more professional looking. Most pantsuits can be worn more than once before cleaning.

A variety of materials have made most pantsuits machine washable and easy to iron. Best of all, it is not necessary to wear pantyhose. Dress socks or knee-high hose are much more comfortable.

There hardly seems to be a cut or design or color that would make the style inappropriate for the office. However, it makes sense that cut-outs, tight-fitting pant legs, and neon colors should be avoided.

Dresses with jackets work fine for the office as well. Solid colors or small prints work well in a professional atmosphere.

Length of the dress or skirt should be just below or at the knee; otherwise, the constant tugging can be annoying.

Just about any style is acceptable so long as it does not show too much leg, shoulder, or bosom or is generally too tight.

Clothes must be clean, pressed, and well fitting. Same thing goes for uniforms.

Fit is particularly important when it comes to making a competent, trustworthy, knowledgeable appearance.

EX: *I had a very dear friend that I met for lunch often. Like most women, we enjoyed looking and commenting on passersby as we ate. She had a curt remark that she would say about a person in the middle of our conversation, "She must not have a mirror in her house!" and then calmly go on with our chat.*

The first time she said that I was caught off guard and replied, "What?" She would nod her head at the passerby, and then I caught it. The person was not well put together in some way that surely a look in the mirror would have shown.

The last thing to do before leaving the house? Look in the mirror!

****

Breakdown of Generations by Age Groups

For statistical purposes, generations have been broken into groups. Most of us were taught that a generation spans twenty-five years. However, a breakdown of groups is shorter, perhaps for compatibility. Each group covers from fifteen to eighteen years.

The generation above the Baby Boomers is labeled the Greatest Generation, and these individuals are mostly retired. Baby Boomers were born between 1946 and 1964, getting close to retirement, ages from fifty-seven to seventy-five, a span of eighteen years. Gen X were born between 1965 and 1979, a span of fifteen years. Millennials were born between 1981 and 1994, a span of fifteen years. Gen Z was born between 1997 and 2012, a span of eighteen years. Of the four groups, the Baby Boomers and the Millennials are the largest.

In business and daily lifestyles, these groups trend in opposite directions. Baby Boomers lean more conservative, holding to certain values that they learned from their parents. Millennials lean more liberal, shaking off some of their parents' ideas and values. They feel government should offer more in social services and are concerned about LGBT members of our society.

Both groups being almost equal in size show a healthy mix of ideas in the workplace.

Group	Dates	Age	How Many
Baby Boomer	1946–1964	57–75	71.6 Million
Gen X	1965–1979	41–56	65.2 Million
Millennials	1981–1994	25–40	72.1 Million
Gen Z	1997–2012	6–24	68 Million

You will be seeing these designations several times in this next section.

Motivations for Opening a Business

People have a variety of reasons for deciding to go out on their own and start a business instead of working for someone else. Of those surveyed, the following reasons are the most often cited. They are listed from the most often to the least often.

Ready to be their own boss	29%
Dissatisfied With Corporate America	17%
Want to pursue personal passion	16%
Opportunity Presented itself	12%

Inspiration for new business	9%
Not ready to retire	7%
Laid off/job outsourced	7%

Managing a Work/Life Balance for Working Moms

Working mothers worry over how to have it all. Many try to figure out how to wear the proverbial two hats, the mom hat and the business hat.

Modern society argues over whether women can "have it all," that is, being a full-time mom and a full-time businesswoman.

Some mothers feel guilty when they are at work and not at home, and vice versa. Personally, I do not think moms should waste valuable time feeling guilty about what they call their double life. When in most households today, both mom and dad work. And both parents must share child rearing tasks.

Just being a mother translates to wearing many hats. Think if it this way: The average family has two or three children. We will go with three. One is a toddler, another is a second grader, and the third one is late for soccer practice.

At this very minute, the toddler needs a dry diaper, the second grader is in tears about some unknown but dire calamity, and the teenager is in a fit because he is late for practice and might get benched.

All three problems need immediate attention, and Mom is only one person. What to do? Mom diapers the toddler, wipes the tears away and soothes the second grader, piles all three in the car, and breaks the speed limit to get her soccer player to practice.

She secretly pulls the coach aside to explain why her son was late to practice and on the way home decides what the family is going to have for dinner.

Dad will pick up the soccer player, so Mom has some breathing space to concentrate on dinner.

Dad and the teenager get home, Mom is putting the finishing touches on dinner, Dad pops into his den to drop off his briefcase, and after a brief rough-housing between Dad and the kids, they all sit down to eat.

Who but a mom could handle all that hubbub, straighten it out, and move forward without having a meltdown herself? Nobody but another mom.

Mom really wears two hats, a work hat and a home hat. The question remains. Can women have it all? A career and a family? **I think that women have proved that they can.**

They must be organized, and they need to include their spouse and the children in managing the home. After all, the home front belongs to all.

Working mothers must keep in mind that they cannot do everything at once. To keep some semblance of sanity in their lives, women must know their priorities.

Do what feels right. Outsource when possible. Share chores with spouse. Involve the children in some chores. Do not try to do everything without help.

Do not carry over from work to home and vice versa. Be 100 percent when at work and 100 percent when at home.

Finally, stop trying to find a true work/life balance. In my estimation, there is no such thing. The balance will fluctuate from one side to the other.

12

Steps to Rebuild a Small Business

After the Pandemic:

Consumers will expect more strict cleanliness standards: businesses will be expected to put the customers health and safety first.

Virtual fitness and training are here to stay. People will continue to access health services.

Even though the general mandate on wearing masks has been lifted, some will continue to wear them, and social distancing may be the norm for some time.

Technology will play an increasingly important role in health issues.

How to Rebuild a Small Business

If you had a small business venture up and running before the pandemic, can you revive it and start over again?

The pandemic will not last forever; the new normal will fade, and most Americans will go back to business as usual.

Some things will never be the same: lives were lost, jobs were wiped out, companies went into bankruptcy, and the future looks uncertain. But look on the bright side: as a beleaguered business owner, the ball is in your court.

What to Do, Where to Start?

First, start by getting the money to restart.

It is highly likely owners were wiped out financially and will need money to start over. The Small Business Administration (SBA) has several loan packages to match whatever your needs are.

1. Paycheck Protection Program
2. Economic Injury and Disaster loan
3. Emergency Economic Injury
4. SBA Disaster Relief
5. SBA Express Bridge Loans

Second, redo your business plan. Due to Covid-19, your business plan has become obsolete, or maybe you never got around to writing one before; it is imperative that you write one now.

1. Define your business current situation: what is broken, what is not.
2. Determine your goals: twelve months, three years, five years.
3. Analyze the state of your industry and customers. Revisit customer base—are their needs the same? Or different?
4. Check your direct and indirect competitors.
How will you make your goals a reality? Reclaiming lost clients? money for rebuilding?
6. Transform knowledge into business plan—all knowledge, tactics, and answers into one formalized plan with everything from executive plans to financial strategy.

Rebuilding will be hard—it will take everything—time, money, and all the blood, sweat, and tears that were used the first time.

The pandemic is on its way out—if you have not started rebuilding yet, get busy fast.

1. Secure financing,
2. Rebuild your team—get as many workers back as possible.
3. Reclaim your customers.
4. Restock inventory.
5. Cut wasted expenses—go lean—establish a frugal mindset.
6. Diversify your products and services, add additional services.
7. Identify opportunities.
8. Remember lessons learned—what went well, what did not.

9. Give back to the community.
10. Prepare for the next disaster—anything can happen.
11. Remember where you fell short this time.
12. Explore everything from the SBA all types of loans, not only government-funded but also government-backed.

America runs on Small Business: customers, employers, community.

Small Business Short Terms

Women Owned Small Business (WOSB):

A WOSB is a small business concern that is at least 51 percent directly and unconditionally owned and controlled by one or more women who are citizens (born or naturalized) of the United States.

Best businesses for a woman: ones that involve the dot-com industry, or the Internet. Virtual services, administrative assistant, advertising, web designer, stores that sell products, personal and skin care.

Percentage of women business owners

What percentage of businesses are owned by women? 36 percent of all businesses are women owned. Those businesses account for 12 percent of all sales and 15 percent of employment. Two point five million businesses are owned equally by women and men.

What is a female minority-owned business?

A business that is at least 51 percent owned and controlled by one or more minority persons.

Statistics of Women in Business

Over eleven million women are in the workforce.

Thirty-nine percent of all US businesses have majority ownership, employ nearly nine million people, and generate more than $1.7 trillion in revenue.

Women are the sole source of income in 40 percent of all households and outpace men in educational achievement.

Becoming Certified for the Women-Owned Small Business Federal Contracting Program

Means a business is eligible to compete for set-aside government contracts within eligible industries.

In 2019 prime contracts were awarded to fifteen thousand WOSB, with an average award of $1.85 million per prime contractor.

13

Small Business Re-Cap 2019–2021

Small Business and Covid-19

The 2020 pandemic had major impacts on small business. Twenty-three percent reported that they had experienced a loss of revenue, while 6 percent reported increased revenue.

Eleven percent reduced their budgets, while another 11 percent temporarily closed their businesses.

Ten percent of owners cut their own wages and the balance of employers laid off or furloughed employees.

Seven percent of small businesses temporarily modified their business models to new practices such as remote-work forces, curbside pick-up, delivery, and other social distancing practices.

When asked if they had implemented innovative changes in their businesses because of the pandemic, 41 percent said that they had. These ranged from adding new hands-free systems to moving to digital marketing to adding new product lines.

These variations and innovations show the resilience of small business to continue to provide services and products to customers despite Covid-19.

Five Most Common Negative Impacts on Business from Covid-19

Percentage of those surveyed

Loss of Revenue	23%
Reduced Budget	11%

Temporary Closing	11%
Cut Wages	10%
Temporary Pivot	7%

Covid-19 Did Impact Small Businesses in the Profit Area

Nineteen percent of businesses reported a profit loss in 2019. Sixty-three percent reported a profit in 2020.

Despite Covid's impact, 78 percent of small business owners expect their businesses to survive the pandemic, while only 4 percent expect their businesses to fail.

While nobody can be sure of what will happen in late 2020 and 2021, small business owners are hard to discourage.

The stimulus loans from the federal government have given owners hope that they can make it through covid soon.

Top Non-Covid Business Challenges—2020

Lack of Capital	23%
Recruit/Retain Employees	19%
Marketing/Adv	15%
Time Management	14%
Admin Work	13%
Manage/Covid Benefits	8%
Other	7%

Small Business in 2021

What does small business look like halfway through 2021? Thirty-one percent of small businesses have been opened for a decade or more. Nineteen percent have been in operation for one year or less, and the other 19 percent have been in operation for two to three years.

Most business owners (58 percent) started a new, independent business from scratch, 18 percent bought an independent business, 19 percent invested in a brand-new franchise, while 6 percent bought an existing location.

Year after year, the number of new franchises has nearly doubled, pointing to the popularity of that business model.

The big challenge is financing, with cash being the most popular form. Rollovers for business startups, also known as 401K business financing, is popular.

Aid from friends and family is also a common way to get started, while SBA loans and lines of credit are used by about 9 percent.

The food and restaurant businesses account for one of the most popular industries for small business. Retail stores, including eCommerce and business services, were the next most popular industries.

Health, beauty, and fitness businesses were next, with finance, insurance, and law rounding out the balance of small businesses surveyed.

Twenty-three percent of small businesses are solo enterprises, run by the business owner alone; 44 percent have two to five employees; 17 percent have six to ten employees; and only 1 percent of small businesses have over one hundred employees.

Confidence in Small Business in Today's Political Climate

Percentage of those surveyed

2021

No Confidence	16%
Little Confidence	26%
Neutral	22%
Somewhat Confident	37%
Very confident	22%

2020

No Confidence	8%
Little Confidence	11%
Neutral	21%
Somewhat Confident	29%
Very Confident	8%

14

Women Small Business Owners

Small business owners in 2021

The number of women small business owners has been increasing every year, but 2020 registered the greatest increase over the last few years. Female business owners increased by 13 percent. The majority of owners remains at 68 percent men, with women now at 32 percent.

There has been a shift of Baby Boomers (41 percent) from small business owners to Gen X (46 percent). As of now, Millennials make up 13 percent of small business owners, while only 1 percent are Gen Z, or Zoomers.

The motivation for starting their own businesses are mostly common themes that have been cited before: want to be their own boss, dissatisfaction with corporate America, to pursue their own passion.

Challenges faced by owners, other than the pandemic, are a lack of capital or cash flow, recruiting and keeping employees, marketing and advertising, managing and benefits.

Despite the pandemic and other challenges, most small business owners are ready to move on with their business.

Owners (51 percent) are primarily interested in growing their business. Thirty percent are focused on sustaining their current business, and 10 percent want to open a new location, while 9 percent are interested in selling their business.

Small business owners are considering several ideas for expanding their businesses such as digital marketing along with traditional marketing, recruiting staff and remodeling, investing in IT infrastructure business services.

Political unrest across the country has had its effect on small business owners as well, resulting in a range of mixed feelings about the effect of politics on businesses.

Business owners were asked who they voted for, and 43 percent said Trump, while 42 percent said Biden. The remaining 15 percent said "other" or "Libertarian" or "no one."

There was a range of feelings on whether they were confident or unconfident about the effects of politics on business. There were mixed feelings, but a small percent felt confident over those who chose to be unconfident.

Finally, when asked about topics that were most important to them, business taxes were at the top of the list, followed by Covid-19-related issues, healthcare, economic relief, and interest rates.

Women in Small Business

About 40 percent of women business owners feel less than confident about the fate of small business in a post-Covid world and 44 percent feel somewhat to very confident.

Sixteen percent are neutral. Women business owners did take a hit during the pandemic. Over 21 percent incurred revenue loss; 12 percent closed their businesses temporarily; 11 percent reduced their budget; 9 percent cut their own wages; 11 percent laid off employees. However, less than one percent were forced to close for good.

Nevertheless, women owners are getting creative. They have made changes in how they handle goods and services, among other things.

Despite the challenges they have endured from Coved 19 throughout 2020, 77 percent expect their businesses to survive beyond Covid-19.

Expectations are looking up for 2021. Nearly half of women business owners plan to grow their current location, 9 percent plan to sell, and 8 percent plan to open a second location.

Some have big plans to invest. Eighty-three percent plan to invest in digital or traditional marketing; 44 percent will remodel or expand; 43 percent will increase staff.

In the end, 76 percent report being somewhat or very happy, while just 14 percent report being unhappy. Despite all the challenges and setbacks of 2020, women business owners are moving up.

Women Business Owners—Generational Breakdown

Gen Z	1%
Boomers	17%
Millennials	31%
Gen X	51%

Black Women Small Business Owners

Black entrepreneurs are an essential part of the small business economy. Women make up 46 percent of black small business owners—this is the highest percentage of owners in any segment. In this group, 33 percent have bachelor's degrees and 26 percent have master's degrees.

Black small business owners are, on average, younger than their white peers. Twenty-seven percent are boomers, 49 percent are Gen X, 21 percent are Millennials, 3 percent are Gen Z.

A majority of Black small business owners are happy in their role as entrepreneurs. Cash is the most popular business funding option for Black owners.

The vast majority (77 percent) of Black business owners started their own new independent business rather than starting or buying a franchise location or an existing business.

Their biggest struggle over the past twelve months has been lack of capital due to Black businesses being concentrated in hard-hit service industries and the problems of equitably receiving funding and financial aid.

Despite the problems of Covid-19, a majority of Black business owners (55 percent) want to grow their business rather than just sustaining it, selling it, or opening in a new location. Sixty-one percent plan to expand or remodel in 2021; 51 percent plan to invest in digital marketing, and 46 percent plan to hire more staff.

With more governmental assistance and a determined attitude for future success, Black-owned small businesses will sustain themselves through 2021 and hopefully begin to rebuild for the future.

Percentage of Black Small Business Owners
Generational Breakdown—Percentage of those surveyed

Boomers	27%
Millennials	4%
Gen X	49%
Gen Z	-3%

15

Rewrite Your Resume for the Post-Covid Job Market

In this last year and a half, businesses have disappeared, others are hanging on by a thread, and some are thriving. This is the time to review your job situation.

Are you comfortable with your current employment? Or are you looking for something better?

Before answering those questions, look at your resume and bring it up to date. In an uncertain market, now is the time to become inventive. Put together a resume that shows you are ready for any opportunity and have the necessary skills to make new things happen.

Add any new skill that you have gained this past year to your resume. It can be a technical skill or a skill that is hard to find, even a skill learned from a new hobby.

If you volunteered during the pandemic or took care of family members, add that to your resume—detailing your accomplishments and responsibilities.

Save some finer points about what you learned for a possible second or follow-up interview.

To slip past the tracking systems that are looking for the most qualified applicants, try using keywords directly in your resume that were used in the job description.

Explain any gaps in your employment. If you took time off to help an ailing relative or you were laid off because of closings due to the pandemic, explain exactly why. A recruiter will likely understand if you are forthright.

Exhibit skills that highlight your talents off the paper. For instance, if you are a writer, show clips of your recent material.

Think of these exhibits as proof of your skill.

Finally, keep your resume simple and organized. No distracting fonts or other embellishments. These just complicate the resume and makes a poor impression on the recruiter.

16

The Future of Women in Business

Women outnumbered men in the work force in 2019 for the second time in history. The first time was in 2010, right after the great recession.

The US Bureau of Labor Statistics reports that in 2019 the total non-farm payroll employment was 145,000. Women took 139,000 of those jobs, or 50.04 percent. Figures have not yet been compiled for 2020 and the Covid-19 crisis; however, the shift toward more women in the workforce is expected to continue to increase.

More and more women are getting college degrees. Women received more bachelor's degrees than men for the first time in 1981. The trend is growing. Women earned 57 percent of all degrees earned in 2017.

Women are taking over professions that were traditionally held by males. That brings a healthy mix of representation in all areas of business.

Female-dominated industries are growing fast: healthcare, marketing, business administration, tech, and even law. More and more roles will be changing as time moves on. Women now make up a majority of HR professionals, managers, and senior leaders.

The make-up and needs of families have changed over the years. It is no longer the norm to expect a household to run on a single income. The US Bureau of Labor Statistics shows that in 2018 48.8 percent of families in the country were two-income families.

Conclusion

I received this in my email July 4, 2021. It makes a good conclusion for **Women in the Job Market, 10 Ways to Balance Work and Home, and More.**

What is happening in the post-Covid work world because of isolation and uncertainty?

Being in lockdown for roughly a year and a half has caused some unusual behavior in workers returning to their jobs. They have been quitting in record numbers.

In April alone, four million US workers quit their jobs. It appears to be a global phenomenon, with a staggering 40 percent of the global workforce considering leaving their jobs this year. Burnout is being cited as the biggest reason for the job exodus. One of the ways people deal with burnout is to change employers.

But burnout alone cannot be the only reason. The job market was experiencing burnout before the pandemic. During the pandemic, workers had time—too much time—to think about what is valuable to them and the place of work in their lives. They have had time to decide what they wanted to leave behind with the pandemic and what they wanted to bring with them into the post-pandemic future.

While people were cut off from the outside world, they began to consider success in different ways. They are looking for different, more fulfilling ways of achieving success. Now, millions of workers are coming out of the pandemic even more anxious and depressed than before.

Many are feeling desperate for a change in their lives, and the easiest thing to change is their job. Many are overwhelmed by things that they cannot control, so they focus on whatever they can control.

Employers have no choice but to respond in some way to this new phenomenon. It is not going to be about perks like things or elaborate buffets but rather introducing mental, emotional, and physical well-being.

It is not about working hard and burning out; it is more about being recharged so that workers can show up at their best, most productive, most creative selves. Recharging is the foundation of any strategy for both a broader definition of success on the personal level and a sustainable definition of success for business.

It is encouraging that companies are recognizing the importance of well-being and the dangers of burnout. But people have been burning out for years. They take some time off to rejuvenate and then come back to burn out again. What has changed now is that the lows have gotten more extreme.

This is a once-in-a-generation opportunity to redefine success and the way we work and live right along with it. People are waking up to realize that burnout is not always the price they should have to pay for success. Companies that realize this will be less likely to capsize over a great wave of resignations.

A survey by the American Psychological Association found that about half of Americans are anxious about resuming in-person interaction. About 72 percent say they are already burned out. What can we do to counteract this cycle? Perhaps we should start by taking small steps toward adequate sleep, better nutrition, and taking baby steps to focus on creativity and purpose.

The End

Sources

Website: Affiliate Marketing for Busy Moms – Barbara Nelson

5 Make-up Tips for Professional Women – Julia Layton

GuidantFinancial.com/Small -business-trends/

Guidantfinancial.com/small-business-trends/women-in-business/.

Guidantfinancial.com small-business-trends/African Americans-in –business/

Lean N.org

Forbes

A Case for the Hybrid Work Model. Lisa Walker, LinkedIn

HR Dive Ryan Golden

US Chamber of Commerce—Changes in Small Business by Nicole Fallan

Guide to Rebuilding your Small Business After the Pandemic by Jessie
Sumrak

GSA Government Blog

Huffington Post Johnson Hur

BeBusinessED.com

Smithsonian Institute Livia Gershan

National Restaurant Association

The Future of Business: More Women in the Workforce, Julie Bawden-Davis,
writer/author Garden Guides Press

US Bureau of Labor Statistics

Experian.com/small business/matters/2018/ 01/29/Statistics

5 Tips for Refreshing Your Resume 06/20/21 St. Louis Post Dispatch,
Diana Shi

St. Louis Post Dispatch, Arianna Huffington,

On My Mind 07/4/21Thrive Global Holdings

About the Author

I was born on October 15, 1932, in Tampa, Florida, right at the waning of the Great Depression. Times were tough until the United States entered World War Two on December 7, 1941.

My father landed a job at the naval shipyards in Tampa, Florida. He was a boilermaker, and navy ships regularly limped into Tampa Bay for repairs.

He made good money, and my parents were finally able to buy a piece of land and build a small home on the outskirts of Tampa in Hillsborough County.

I walked a mile and a half to school and a mile and a half back home. We had enough property to maintain a large vegetable garden and a large brood of chickens, which provided us with eggs and an occasional platter of fried chicken and all the vegetables we wanted.

Having chickens meant that we bought feed in large bags. Bags those days were good cotton material with printed patterns on them. Mom washed the bags, ironed the material, and made dresses, skirts, and blouses for me and for her. Everybody did.

After the war, the country was in good financial condition, and people were able to buy homes, new cars, invest money, send their kids to college. After high school, I attended Tampa University and majored in voice. While in college, I worked part time in retail.

Married in 1954 and had one son in 1957.

My husband was a geologist. We moved from Tampa to Colorado to Idaho until he was hired at St. Louis Community College here in St. Louis.

We moved from Idaho to St. Louis in 1964. I taught music for three or four years in St. Louis. Even though I had gone to college earlier, I had never finished. Concordia University of Wisconsin had a satellite program in St. Louis, and I graduated with a Bachelor of Arts degree in 1996.

I was a news editor and on-air news person for radio stations KFUOAM and FM in St. Louis for ten years. Worked for The Lutheran Church—Missouri Synod as editor of the **Saint Louis Lutheran** for four years and then took a job as an organist for Prince of Peace Lutheran Church for twenty-three years until I retired. I continued to work part time after retirement as a substitute organist until the beginning of the pandemic when churches were shut down.

Joined online *Wealthy Affiliate* and created a website on the care of pets.

Set up a second website on *Affiliate Marketing for Busy Moms*. Discovered tending to two websites was too much so I let the Busy Mom site lay dormant.

This year I decided to make use of the material I had written for the Busy Mom site to write and compile a book for women trying to get back into the job market after the pandemic.

It has not always been easy making a living. But it has been an interesting voyage, and I have learned a lot of things I never would have if life had been easy. *Barbara Leist Nelson*

Appendix

Since I am affiliated with *Wealthy Affiliate*, it seemed proper to let my readers know about it. It is a good choice for people who can wait for a while before seeing any compensation while building a business that will bring in a good steady passive income. WealthyAffiliate.com will get you there.

Wealthy Affiliate is an internet company formed about fifteen years ago by two Canadians. WA teaches participants how to build and maintain a website, write content on a particular subject, and connect with affiliate companies who pay a commission to owners of these websites for merchandise sold.

Presently, Wealthy Affiliate has over a million participants. One of the perks is, if you maintain your membership, your website is on WA's platform free. All you pay for each year is the domain, which is $14.99 and your membership.

The lessons and materials are available for newcomers and long-time members on a continuous basis. New material is presented all the time. Lessons are presented in video and in text. WA adheres to a pay-it-forward attitude for all members. Members help other members without expecting payback. If you have been assisted in any way, you simply pay it forward by assisting someone else.

For those who really want to set up a passive income business and are willing to wait for six months to a year before seeing any income, this is one internet company to investigate.

It is on the level; people who have stayed the course are making good money. The hard work is up front; the money comes later. It is a bona fide organization. It is not a scam. People who are savvy about the internet do the best.

www.ingramcontent.com/pod-product-compliance
Lightning Source LLC
Chambersburg PA
CBHW061515180526
45171CB00001B/187